SUPER SIMPLE STORY STRUCTURE

A QUICK GUIDE TO PLOTTING & WRITING YOUR NOVEL

L. M. LILLY

WRITING AS A SECOND CAREER

INTRODUCTION

In the fiction writing classes I took in college (I majored in Writing/English), the word "plot" was barely spoken. We learned to write vivid scenes, and our instructors said that to write a novel we should just string those scenes together. I discovered that's not as easy as it sounds, at least not if you want a good story that keeps readers turning pages.

So I learned how to construct a plot the hard way, by writing several novels that didn't work, despite that they included vivid scenes. After studying different plot structures and experimenting a lot, I finally figured out an approach—the Super Simple Story Structure—that allows for faster writing, minimizes the need for major rewrites, and keeps readers turning the pages.

By sharing it, I'm hoping I'll save you from needing to write four novels that don't work before you write one that does.

In the pages that follow, we'll walk through five simple steps, the same ones I've used for every novel I've published.

What you'll create won't be so structured that you feel hemmed in and stifled, but it will be enough that you can write your first draft quickly, without getting stuck staring at a blank screen for an hour, then giving up and checking your social media accounts.

Before you take my advice, though, you might want to know a little more about my writing career.

Learn From My Mistakes (And Successes)

My first published novel, **The Awakening**, is Book 1 in a four-book supernatural thriller series. **The Awakening** has been downloaded over 50,000 times and has reached No. 1 in numerous categories for free and paid books on Amazon, including Occult, Horror, Feminist, and Paranormal. The fourth and final book is being released May 15, 2017. All the books are (or will be) available on multiple platforms in ebook, paperback, and audiobook editions. My other published work includes a standalone supernatural suspense novel, a short story collection, and a non-fiction book on the Supreme Court. (I'm also a lawyer.)

The first novel I wrote met with no success at all. I followed my teachers' advice and strung a bunch of scenes together. It was an autobiographical young adult novel, a genre I don't write in anymore, and it covered a year in the life of a thirteen-year-old girl. Unfortunately for my writing (though probably not for my life), I wasn't a very edgy kid. All the characters were pretty nice, and there simply wasn't enough conflict.

As I'll talk about in Chapter One, without conflict there's no story, so that was a problem.

Trying to ensure conflict, next I wrote a problem novel. It was about a freshman in high school whose best friend was an alcoholic. After writing a hundred pages, I realized all of what I'd written was unnecessary backstory and threw it out. I did finish the novel, but I regretted the waste of time, especially because I had so little of it to spare.

Back then, the only way to sell a novel and have anyone but your family and best friend buy it was to get a publisher to publish it. The agents and publishers I wrote to sent me nothing but form letter rejections for those two novels. (They sent actual letters on paper back then. Once, after having been particularly industrious sending out queries, I opened my mailbox to find 50 rejection letters. That was a really fun day.)

After the two tries at winging it, I plotted my next novel in detail. For every scene in every chapter, I wrote a page describing what would happen. That left me feeling hemmed in and not all that creative, but it was the first manuscript that got me personal letters and encouragement from editors.

That's when I started reading books on screenwriting, attending workshops where the instructors focused on plot, and seeking help from a screenwriter friend. It took yet another novel (I'm a slow learner), but I finally figured out the steps that worked, which I'll share with you. The Super Simple Story Structure not only made my books into page-turners, it allowed me to write much faster.

I'll walk you through it step-by-step.

Step One will help you figure out where to start your novel and what it's about. In Step Two, you'll learn to create five basic plot points. Steps

Three and Four cover subplots and winding up your novel. In Step Five, just before you start writing, we'll talk about your point of view options. I'll end with tips on how to write your novel quickly.

I recommend reading with a pen and paper, your keyboard, or your phone at your side so you can write answers to the questions and prompts that are provided (designated with a *), or at least start making notes.

If you prefer, you can buy the paperback workbook edition or download free story structure worksheets at WritingAsASecondCareer.com/Your-Novel to fill in.

You should also feel free to read the entire book once, then go back and fill in the blanks to plot your novel.

Books, Films, and Spoilers

Throughout this book, I use examples from **Gone With The Wind** (the book and the film), **The Terminator** (the original film and my personal favorite movie of all time), and, to a lesser extent, **Terminator 2: Judgment Day**. I chose these three because they're well-known stories, the plots are clear, and most people are already familiar with them.

There are serious issues with the way **Gone**

With The Wind portrays slavery, the Confederacy, and the KKK to list only a few issues. I've used it not because I agree with its slant but because the plot turns are so strikingly clear. You need not read or watch it if you'd rather not — this book explains what you'll need to know.

I also use examples from my first two supernatural thrillers, **The Awakening (Book 1)** and **The Unbelievers (The Awakening Book 2)**, because I know firsthand what factored into the writing process. When I look at other writers' work, I'm reasoning backward from what I see to their process. With **The Awakening Series**, I can tell you not only what I was doing, but why.

Other books and films are mentioned as well, but nothing that will spoil anything if you haven't read or seen them yet.

I deliberately drew from different types of stories in different genres, so you can see that the Super Simple Story Structure works regardless. Whatever type of novel you want to write, it can work for you too.

You don't need to have read or watched any of these novels or films to learn from the examples, though you may want to if you'd like to see how specific plot points fit within the entire plots. (And, obviously, far be it from me to discourage anyone from reading one of my novels.)

Okay, ready?

We'll begin with the Cardinal Rule of writing a good story. Here's a hint: if you're a fictional character, you can't always get what you want.

1
STEP ONE: IN THE BEGINNING THERE WAS CONFLICT

Before you put pen to page or hands to keyboard, and before you start thinking about your novel's plot points, there is one thing absolutely every novel needs:

Conflict.

I'll be using the word a lot because it's what's most often missing in first chapters by new writers. Even with experienced writers, a weak conflict is usually at the heart of a book that loses the reader's interest halfway through.

That's why Step One is creating or discovering your conflict.

Where does conflict start? With your two major characters, the protagonist and antagonist.

We'll get to them, but first, a little more on the cardinal rule. Which is, you guessed it, conflict.

The Cardinal Rule

If you've ever watched a soap opera, daytime or otherwise, you've witnessed the cardinal rule at work. It applies to any drama or comedy, but it's most obvious in television shows. **Once a character reaches a moment of happiness, that character disappears until things go wrong again.**

If everyone's happy, or at least content, the reader or watcher isn't interested. **Without conflict, there's no story.** There's no suspense, no question that keeps the reader turning pages in the hope of an answer, and no one to root for or against. This is true whether you're writing a novel, telling a ghost story around a campfire, or improvising a skit at your local comedy club.

The best way to have a strong conflict is for your main character to want something that is hard to achieve.

As an example, through almost all of **Gone With The Wind**, Scarlett O'Hara is madly in love with Ashley Wilkes and wants him to love and marry her. There are many obstacles, some present from Day One, others that develop:

- He and Scarlett are unsuited to one another. She's driven, ambitious, outspoken, high-spirited, and has little interest in book learning; he prefers a quiet and scholarly life, is reserved, refined, and has little interest in starting a business or earning money;
- Ashley gets engaged to his cousin (Melanie), which is a family tradition;
- Scarlett marries Melanie's brother on the rebound and is quickly widowed, limiting her social interactions, and bonding her to Melanie;
- The Civil War begins, and Ashley leaves to fight in it, perhaps never to return;
- Scarlett marries two more times, the third time to the smart, powerful, and sharp-eyed Rhett Butler;
- Ashley feels at loose ends in the post-war world, where Scarlet flourishes;
- While he's attracted to Scarlett, Ashley truly loves Melanie, though it takes forever for him, and for Scarlett, to realize it.

Any one of these obstacles would be daunting, but Scarlett is faced with all of them.

As **Gone With The Wind shows, life should be hard for your main character.** Resist the temptation to allow your protagonist smooth sailing, or to make things easy. Instead, think about how things can get worse.

If one of your main characters is boring, you probably don't have enough conflict. Conflict needs to be there from the first page. That means as soon as we see your protagonist, that person must want something. It doesn't need to be the main goal that will drive the entire book, but it must be something not immediately available.

For example, though there's nothing about Ashley on the first page of **Gone With The Wind**, nor about the upcoming Civil War, we learn in the second paragraph that Scarlett's nature—willful, outspoken, and "lusty with life"—is "distinctly at variance with her decorous demeanor" and the strictures Southern society places on women. So right away we learn Scarlett wants to be herself and enjoy life, and her culture opposes her. Because there's immediate conflict, the reader is willing to wait a while as the larger conflicts, both personal and societal, unfold.

That doesn't mean your first scene needs to include your protagonist—the main character who is the focus of the story—though most novels do. But it is your protagonist's conflict that will drive the story, so we'll start there.

2

YOUR PROTAGONIST

A lot of writers start with a main character or a set of characters about whom they feel strongly or with whom they empathize. I began my first novel, the autobiographical one, that way. I named the character Katie, the name my mother told me I wished I'd been named when I was a kid. (My novels got a lot better when I stopped using myself as a model, but that's another issue.)

You may have in mind a main character of a particular age, occupation, personality, or family situation, and those things are important. But one thing is more important: **What does your protagonist want?**

Your Protagonist's Goal

Your protagonist must have a goal that is large enough and difficult enough to reach that she or he will be facing obstacles until the end of the novel.

* In other words, at the end of the novel, where does your protagonist desperately want or need to be?

If your protagonist doesn't want anything, you don't have a story. So you'll need to figure out what she or he wants, create a goal, or choose a new protagonist.

Not only must your protagonist have a goal, but there must be a strong reason to want it, otherwise the story will fall flat. **In short, the protagonist must care.**

If my main character's goal is to get into a summer internship program in Boston at a brokerage firm, but she'd be equally happy to live with her parents all summer and work with her friends as a lifeguard at the local pool, the story won't be compelling. If she doesn't care, neither will the reader.

On the other hand, if her student loans are coming due, after thirty interviews she hasn't gotten a single job offer, she's always wanted to live in Boston, and the internship has a good chance of leading to full-time employment, now we have a goal she (and the reader) will care about. If you want to up the stakes, let's say her parents both got laid off from their jobs last year and were forced to downsize and move to a one-bedroom apartment in a state with a lower cost of living. She's sleeping on the couch and living far from any urban area with the types of jobs that she trained for, and she can only afford plane tickets to this one last interview.

Now we really have a conflict.

Go back to your protagonist and think about why she or he wants to reach the goal. What life circumstances make it vital? What about his or her personality contributes to the longing to achieve this?

* Why does your protagonist want to reach this goal?

Active v. Passive

To be engaging, your protagonist must strive for her or his goal. That doesn't mean you need a superhero for a main character. In fact, as we'll talk about in the next chapter, in a battle with the antagonist, your protagonist generally should be the underdog. It does mean your protagonist must do as much as she or he possibly can to move forward within the limits of the world and the character you've created.

In the first half of **The Terminator**, from an action hero perspective, Sarah Connor is not particularly active. She doesn't know how to fight or have any special skills or knowledge. But for who she is and where she is in life, she does everything she can.

When she's out at a bar and grill and sees a television news report that two women named Sarah Connor have been murdered, she immediately tries to call the police. The payphone, the only option in the 80s for calling when you're away from home, is broken. She's made a big deal about seeing the news report, which might make it obvious she's worried. So Sarah leaves the bar and grill, blending with a crowd and staying alert. When she realizes someone is following her, she enters a nightclub, paying a cover charge just to get in and use the payphone. She persists in trying to reach the correct person at the police station despite being transferred all over, follows the instructions she gets, follows the instructions of a stranger, Kyle Reese, when he's able to fend off the Terminator, and listens to Reese's explanation despite how crazy it sounds.

In other words, Sarah Connor is the opposite of the idiot in the horror movie who is alone in a strange house at night, hears noises coming from the attic, and heads right up the stairs to have her throat slit.

There Can Be Only One

A novel should have one and only one protagonist, though there can be multiple characters the reader identifies with and cares about. When I was outlining **The Awakening**, my initial plan was to have six main characters, each of whom discovered she was pregnant despite that being impossible under the usual laws of nature. They were to be of different ages, races, and backgrounds.

I took my idea and outline to a writing retreat and was lucky enough to take part in a session with horror author John Saul and his writing partner. They trounced my idea. They—and everyone in my retreat group—agreed that six pregnant women was five too many. My thriller retreat instructor helped me narrow down to one protagonist and yet keep my theme of women banding together to combat forces that threatened their lives. I chose Tara Spencer as the protagonist. A few of the other women characters morphed into (non-pregnant) allies and friends of Tara.

While I shifted my story idea quite a bit, the premise remained. The book—and eventually the series—focused on a modern-day supernatural pregnancy, a powerful religious cult, and what happens when it turns out the child will be a girl.

As this example shows, if you have a group of characters that call to you, you don't need to change your whole premise. You simply need to figure out which one you care about most. The protagonist also should be the character about which the audience feels the most concern, who drives the plot, and who has the most significant story and character arc.

For instance, in **The Terminator**, Kyle Reese is more physically active than Sarah Connor in the first quarter of the movie. He has the weapons, he actively hunts for Sarah while she remains unaware she's in danger, and he fights off the Terminator in the first encounter. Even later in the narrative, he gives Sarah the information she needs, shows her how to make explosives, and explodes the truck the Terminator drives as we near the movie's climax.

But Reese is not the protagonist. First, we identify more with Sarah, partly because for the vast majority of the audience she is more like an average person. She's a waitress sharing a home with a roommate, not a soldier from the future who spent his entire life hiding and fighting. She is more vulnerable and more of an underdog.

She also has the most dramatic story and character arc—that is, she changes the most. She starts as a not-very-competent waitress and a pretty, upbeat, fun, and nice young woman who seemingly has few major concerns. She ends as a fighter who makes use of every available option and who pushes herself to her limits, ready to fight a war to save humanity.

This is not to say that Kyle Reese doesn't grow or change. He grows emotionally. He moves from hero worshipping his image of Sarah, a feeling he hides behind an intense, angry exterior, to loving her as a real person, which love he expresses to her.

Reese does not have much of a story arc, though. He begins with a mission to protect Sarah and destroy the Terminator, and that remains his mission. He contributes mightily to Sarah's eventual success. In fact, without him, she would have been killed at the nightclub where the Terminator first found her. But Reese doesn't make it to the end. He doesn't face off one-on-one with the Terminator.

In contrast, as the film begins, Sarah Connor has no idea about the threat to humanity or to herself. At the climax, though, the final battle is between Sarah and the Terminator, and she defeats the machine.

Now let's look at **Terminator 2: Judgment Day**, because that tells a story that has three significant characters who could be the protagonist: Sarah Connor, John Connor, or the Terminator, who in this movie has been reprogrammed to help John.

So which is the protagonist? Let's talk about each one:

- **Sarah Connor:**

One of my friends likes **T2** better than **The Terminator** because she likes a strong female lead and sees Sarah as stronger in the second movie. She is, if we're looking at physical strength or how much she does throughout the film compared to in the first one. But given where she started in **The Terminator**, Sarah grew more, and had to push herself far more, in the first film, calling on all her reserves.

In T2, she doesn't have as much of a character arc. From beginning to end she's resourceful and determined, as well as angry and struggling not to fall apart emotionally. (At the very end, after the threat is over, she sounds more stable, but we only hear about that in a closing voiceover.) She also doesn't drive the climax of the film. While she strikes important blows, it is the "good" Terminator who fires the killing shot. Finally, Sarah personally is in less peril and she is less intrinsic to the plot. Skynet now wants to kill John Connor, who will grow up to be a leader, and is less worried about Sarah Connor. All these are reasons why Sarah is not the protagonist of **T2**.

- **John Connor:**

John is a kid, so he's vulnerable and makes a good underdog. He influences the Terminator, trying to teach it ethics, he fights, and he learns that, in fact, his mom is not crazy, and there is a nuclear war coming as well as a rise of the machines. He longs for a father figure throughout the movie and finds it a little bit in the Terminator. But he doesn't have much of a character arc, and his approach to life and problems for the most part stays the same.

The best argument for him being the protagonist is that he starts making some decisions about strategy, rather than merely following Sarah's plans, but he and she share the choices that drive the plot. And while he takes part in the final battle, he isn't able to hurt the new Terminator that's pursuing him.

- **The Terminator:**

The cyborg seems like a strange choice for a protagonist, but he (or it) is the protagonist of **T2**. Unlike in the first movie, here, the original model Terminator is vulnerable. He is older and less advanced than the villain, a new model Terminator. He also has the largest character arc. He starts as a programmed robot that will protect John at all costs, without taking into account whether other humans are hurt. He learns, through John, about why it's important to avoid killing humans whenever he can. He starts by asking why people cry and ends expressing understanding of that and feeling pain at losing John. He fires that last shot against the new model Terminator, sending it into a vat of flames. The Terminator also chooses to sacrifice himself to further protect John. While you can argue he's programmed to do that, he specifically says that he's not.

All this together makes him the protagonist.

T2 is a great example of how multiple characters as a team can be at the heart of your story. But even if, as in **T2**, they are all important, you as the author should focus first on the one you choose as the protagonist. It will affect the choices you make regarding your story as you move forward.

She, He, or It

Most of the time, your protagonist will be a person. As we saw in **T2**, though, the protagonist could be a thing, such as a robot or cyborg, or an animal. Usually if the protagonist is a non-human being, such as a cyborg, that character nonetheless possesses, or evolves into possessing, human-like characteristics. All the same rules regarding protagonists still apply.

In the **T2** example above, the Terminator has a strong goal it literally must achieve based on its programming. It is vulnerable. It has the equivalent of feelings. It grows and changes.

A group or organization technically can be a protagonist. The best examples are television shows that focus on a particular organization. Note, however, that while the protagonist for the entire show may be a police department or a government agency, each episode typically features one specific human protagonist in whom the viewer feels the most invested.

For example, **Star Wars**, the original (now known as **A New Hope**), would not have been nearly as compelling if the protagonist were the Rebel Alliance as a group. What draws the viewer in is the personal story of Luke Skywalker, who knows almost nothing about the rebels when the film starts.

Filling In The Blanks

Now that you know, at least for the big picture, what your protagonist wants, and that the protagonist must be active, it's time to consider **other character traits and information.** If you're stuck, think about what will make things harder for your protagonist.

Don't worry if you can't fill in all the blanks now. Write down what's jumping out at you or the characteristics you think make a difference to your main story, also known as your A Plot. Or, if you'd rather learn more about and/or create your antagonist, which is our next step, you can move on and come back to this section later.

And remember, you can always, always revise later, and you probably will.

* Categories to fill in:

Gender
Age
Sexual Orientation
Education
Family
Friends
Romantic Relationships

Occupation(s)
Race/Ethnicity
Other

* **List some ideas for names** (it's okay to use a placeholder if you're not sure—you can always change later).

* **Now, pick three things that you came up with above that you could change that would make reaching the goal even more important to or more difficult for your protagonist.** (You don't need to be wedded to these three things, but coming up with them will help you brainstorm and ensure you're not making life too easy.)

Now it's time to consider who or what opposes your main character.

That would be your antagonist.

3

YOUR ANTAGONIST

At a writers' conference I attended, Karen Joy Fowler, author of **The Jane Austen Book Club**, said if she didn't push her characters, they'd do nothing but drink coffee and talk about relationships. To avoid that, you need a strong, well-motivated antagonist.

In fact, the antagonist has only one job: to oppose the protagonist.

But the antagonist's reason can't be just that you, the author, need an opposing force. Like your protagonist, your antagonist must want something and have strong reasons for wanting it. If your antagonist is willing to give up without much of a fight, or if your antagonist and protagonist can walk away from one another and both get what they want, you have a weak conflict, or no conflict at all.

For that reason, **your protagonist and antagonist should have mutually exclusive goals.** If one wins, the other necessarily loses. This is what's known as a **locked conflict,** and it's the strongest type of conflict you can create.

For example, in **The Terminator**, the antagonist is master computer network Skynet, working through a cyborg known as the Terminator. Skynet sends the Terminator back in time to kill Sarah Connor. Why? Because she will someday get pregnant and give birth to a child, John Connor, who in the future will lead a human rebellion that can defeat Skynet. Sarah Connor wants to survive and have a normal, happy life. The protagonist and antagonist cannot, by definition, both achieve their goals.

In **Gone With The Wind**, there are two story arcs. Scarlett's battle with the Old Guard of Southern Society as it existed before the war and her relationship with Rhett Butler. Thus, there are two antagonists—the Old Guard, expressed through different people in Scarlett's family and community—and Rhett himself. Scarlett wants to prosper financially and determine her own life. The Old Guard wants her to be a proper Southern woman who relies on men (or at least pretends to rely on them) to take care of her. These goals are mutually exclusive. As to her personal story, Scarlett wants Ashley as her lover and husband. Rhett wants Scarlett to love only him. These goals are mutually exclusive.

As with the protagonist, the antagonist can be an It or a group or organization. Further, as the above examples show, it's more common to see a group as an antagonist than as a protagonist, as the reader generally doesn't need to care as much about or identify as closely with the antagonist. Note, however, that you need characters who act for or represent the antagonist in those types of stories. In **The Terminator**, much more screen time is devoted to the agent of the antagonist, The Terminator, than to the computer system itself, and The Terminator is what Sarah defeats in the end.

In **Gone With The Wind**, the Old Guard expresses itself through Mammy, through Scarlett's mother and sister, and through Aunt Pittypat, among others, all of whom love Scarlett but often thwart her. It also expresses itself in far more harsh terms through women and men who are actively angry at Scarlett and make clear their disapproval, such as Ashley's sister, India

Wilkes, and Mrs. Merriwether, the matron of society.

In my **Awakening** series, the antagonist is The Brotherhood of Andrew, a religious order that initially believes Tara Spencer will give birth to a messiah. The Order quickly reverses course and sees her as a potential Antichrist, though, on learning her child will be female. In each book, however, the Brotherhood acts through different people, with one particular Brotherhood member serving as the antagonist for that book. I work hard to make that character a rounded, well-developed person whom the reader can understand if not empathize with.

Now think about your antagonist.

* **What does your antagonist want more than anything else?**

Like the protagonist, the antagonist needs strong motivation. Otherwise, it'll be too easy for the protagonist to reach the goal and not much will happen in your book.

* **Why does your antagonist want to reach this goal?**

* **If the antagonist achieves that goal, does it make it impossible for the protagonist to reach her/his/its goal?**

If you answered Yes, move on. If No, at some

point before you start writing, rethink your characters' goals, both your protagonist's and antagonist's. Adjust them so that they are in direct conflict with one another. You can do that now, or you may want to finish reading about the next step, which is creating your story's plot points.

Moving on may be helpful because sometimes it's easier to work backward to the goals and characters you need for the story you feel compelled to tell.

Other Traits And Information

When creating your antagonist, remember, you want to make things hard for your main character. Think about what type of antagonist will make things most difficult.

In **The Terminator**, Sarah Connor is a waitress in her early twenties with no particular technical or fighting skills. Skynet is a self-aware computer system so powerful that in the not-too-distant future it launches a global nuclear war and is on the verge of exterminating all of humanity. It sends a ruthless, nearly indestructible cyborg back in time to kill Sarah. Kyle Reese, the man the Resistance sends to aid Sarah, is not a muscle-man action figure (despite what you may have seen in **Terminator Genisys**). He doesn't show up armed to the teeth. He's too thin, he can't bring weapons with him, and he arrives naked. While the cyborg is ripping someone's heart out, Reese is stealing a pair of pants from a homeless man in an alley.

Even with Reese's help, Sarah is the very definition of an underdog.

You don't need to go that far, but there should be a mismatch. If the aspiring intern I made up (remember her?) worked her way through a decent college and has somewhat better-than-average grades, her potential boss should be someone from a well-to-do family who went to Harvard and Yale, had a 4.0 average, and thinks that everyone who works for the company needs the same type of credentials and background.

Also, **your antagonist should be a real person/character, not a cardboard cut out.** The best villains are those whose motives we understand and for whom we feel some sympathy. In my **Awakening** series, despite that its members oppose Tara and threaten her life, the Brotherhood of Andrew isn't evil. It has a purpose it is pursuing and its members believe what they are doing serves the will of God. Different characters act as the agents of the Brotherhood in the different books, and each one has personal desires and aims that most people can understand. They struggle with their convictions, questioning and trying to do what is right, and they have distinct personalities rather than being mindless followers in an organization on the fringes of traditional religion.

Even the Terminator, despite being a cyborg programmed to kill, has a sense of humor. He also doesn't kill randomly just because he's evil. He does what he needs to do to achieve his goal. Toward the end of the movie, he tells a truck driver to get out of the truck, he doesn't shove him out or kill him solely to commit another heinous act.

This is why it's important to give as much thought to your antagonist as your protagonist.

As before, don't worry if you can't fill in all the blanks now.

* **Fill in what you can for the categories below and move on.**

Gender
Age
Sexual Orientation
Education
Family
Friends
Romantic Relationships
Occupation(s)
Race/Ethnicity
Other
Ideas for names

* As you did with your protagonist, pick three things that you came up with that you could change that would make reaching the goal even more important to your antagonist. (Remember, still an experiment. You can opt not to make any of these changes, so let your mind range free.)

* Before you leave your antagonist, think again about your protagonist. Make a note of anything you want to change to create a greater mismatch between the two.

If you've created two main characters with strong, mutually-exclusive goals, you've got a good conflict and a good start.

Now the question is, how do they go about striving for those goals in a way that keeps the reader fascinated? That's what we'll figure out as we create the five basic plot points you'll need.

4

STEP TWO: THE 5-POINT PLOT

The Goldilocks of Plot Structure
The 5-point framework is the Goldilocks of plotting. It solves the "plotter or pantser" question—that is, which is better: outlining your novel in detail or winging it? It's what ensures you have a story and not merely a collection of scenes.

Once I've decided on the five points listed below, I create my first draft by writing as fast as I can from point to point. That allows me to write quickly because I know where I'm headed, while still giving me freedom to experiment.

The five points:

- Story Spark

- One-Quarter Twist
- Mid-Point
- Three-Quarter Turn
- Climax

I'll walk through these one at a time, but for now, here's a quick overview:

The first point, the **Story Spark**, gets your main plot—also known as the A Plot—rolling. It answers the question most new writers (and some experienced writers) struggle with, which is, exactly where does the story begin? The Story Spark can occur on the first page or later, but not too much later, as we'll see. The **One-Quarter Twist** occurs one fourth of the way through the novel (surprising right?). It's where something outside the protagonist turns the story in a new direction and raises the stakes.

At the **Mid-Point**, the protagonist makes a vow or commitment and/or suffers a major reversal of fortune. The **Three-Quarter Turn** once again sends the plot in a new direction, but rather than being an outside force, it grows directly out of the action the protagonist took at the Mid-Point.

The **Climax** is the point you're probably most familiar with and could identify off the top of your head for every book you've read and movie you've seen. It's the scene at or near the end where everything converges and our conflict is resolved.

As you figure out each one, always keep in mind that cardinal rule: the best way to create a good story is to have a strong conflict. Do that and your story will move forward almost on its own.

If it doesn't, or if you discover your story taking a new direction as you first draft, the good news is **it's much easier to revise five plot points than to rewrite a 20-page scene-by-scene outline.**

So let's start at the beginning, with the Story Spark.

5

THE STORY SPARK

The Story Spark gets the ball rolling. Your protagonist is going along with normal life as a waitress, a student, a Southern Belle and, bam, something changes.

This also is known as the Inciting Incident. It could happen on your first page or somewhere in the first few chapters. It needs to happen early, though, because **it starts the real story**. What comes before is background or backstory, a glimpse into the character's normal life and what happened before this conflict occurred or came to a head.

In a movie, the Story Spark typically occurs within the first ten minutes. In a book, it's often in the first chapter. The classic example is a murder mystery, where we see a dead body on the first page or at end of the first chapter. As we'll see, the scene that contains the Story Spark doesn't need to include the protagonist, though it quite often does. Regardless, without the Spark, there's no story, and no conflict for our protagonist.

In **The Terminator**, Sarah Connor in the Climax will fight the Terminator to the death. The Story Spark occurs in one of the first scenes of the film, when two naked men, one of whom is actually the cyborg we'll come to know as the Terminator, appear on earth amid lightning. This is important because when we switch to our hero, Sarah, happily cruising on her motor scooter on a sunny California day, we already know there's conflict on the way.

In **Gone With The Wind**, though Scarlett is unaware of either at the beginning of the book, the main story will be about her relationship with Rhett Butler and, on a grander scale, about her surviving the Civil War and the death of the pre-war Southern way of life. The Story Spark occurs when Rhett pops up off the couch, having heard Scarlett's unladylike declaration of love for Ashley Wilkes, and Ashley's rejection of her. Rhett laughs, Scarlett throws a vase, and there you have it. The Story Spark for the more sweeping story also occurs at this time. As Rhett and Scarlett spar, the Civil War is declared. Moments later, a blushing beau asks Scarlett to marry him before he goes off to fight.

In **The Awakening**, the Story Spark occurs on the first page, which is not unusual with a thriller or mystery (see above: dead body on page 1). Tara's doctor tells her she's pregnant, despite that she's never had sexual intercourse. Her goal when we start the book is to become a doctor. Her plan is to finish college and be admitted to medical school before marrying her boyfriend, having sex, and risking pregnancy. The very moment we see her, in the first paragraph of the novel, she's encountering the major obstacle:

> Tara folded and unfolded the pink referral slip. Her fingers made sweat marks on the paper. "I can't be pregnant. I haven't had sex."

Right off the bat, Tara must deal with the actual turn her life has taken and struggle to explain it to everyone else in her life. That includes her boyfriend, who knows he can't be the father.

The Tension Before The Spark

Note that in **Gone With The Wind**, unlike in **The Terminator**, there are quite a few scenes before the Story Spark. How does Margaret Mitchell keep readers engaged until then?

Two ways. One, as we talked about in Chapter One, conflict occurs on the very first page—the conflict between Scarlett's nature and the rules imposed upon women in her society. This actually foreshadows both the major story arcs in the book. We see it again when Mammy insists Scarlett eat before the Wilkes' barbecue (where she'll eventually be rejected by Ashley and meet Rhett), so that she'll eat only tiny morsels there and appear ladylike. Mammy achieves this by playing on what Scarlett wants most—Ashley Wilkes—implying that Ashley prefers dainty, birdlike women.

Seeds are also sown about the Civil War in the very first scene. Mitchell doesn't do that by simply telling us war is on the horizon or by giving us a history lesson. Instead, as she weaves in information and descriptions, she frames the prospect of war in a very personal way for our protagonist. Scarlett is talking to twin brothers who both carry a torch for her. She wants to hear about them being thrown out of school (yet another conflict), and they want to talk about war, a subject that bores her. She becomes impatient and insists there won't be any war.

Also, in that very first scene, Scarlett becomes

upset, but hides it, when the twins tell her Ashley is getting engaged to his cousin Melanie. This is yet another conflict that will feed into the larger story arcs.

In contrast, Tara Spencer's ordinary, pre-pregnancy life in **The Awakening** and her goal of becoming a doctor are conveyed not by pages of description or scenes before the Story Spark, but through a debate with her doctor about, first, why Tara can't be pregnant and, second, how it could possibly have happened. This maintains tension as the reader learns about Tara. Once again, conflict drives the scene and keeps the reader engaged. If instead I started with a long description of Tara's typical day at college or pages of narrative about how she's the oldest of four and loves her brothers and sisters like crazy, or how hard she works at her job, most readers would stop reading.

In **The Terminator**, tension is maintained a different way. In the very beginning, there's a brief voiceover about the machines taking over the world, with short scenes of a grim future with machines and cyborgs hunting humans—emphasis on **brief** and **short**. Nothing will kill reader (or viewer) interest faster than a long download of information about the world of the story. In some fantasy novels, readers have a lot of patience for world building, as that's part of what fans love about the genre. Even there, however, if you're a new author it's best to hook your reader early with compelling personal conflict.

After the voiceover, some conflict occurs in Sarah's day-to-day life, such as mixing up orders from customers, a child putting a scoop of ice cream in her uniform pocket, and a call from her roommate's boyfriend. Some of it is played for humor, as when the boyfriend starts sex talk with Sarah, stammers in embarrassment when she pretends to be shocked and not know who it is, then starts the very same lines when the roommate takes the phone.

But mostly tension and viewer interest is maintained by the scenes that are intercut with Sarah's mundane troubles. We see the Terminator pull the list of Sarah Connors from the phone book and murder one of them. We also see Kyle Reese flee from the police, steal clothes and weapons, and start hunting for Sarah. The first time through, we don't know if he's on her side or is another bad guy after her, which adds another story question for which the viewer wants an answer.

Now to your novel. Think about your protagonist's main goal, the one that will take the entire novel to reach (or clearly fail to reach).

* When is the first time something significant happens that blocks that goal and starts the story?

* Does your protagonist encounter this obstacle on page one? If not, why not?

* Even if you don't plan to do it, brainstorm some ways you could rearrange your plot to get that obstacle onto page one.

* If you're picturing your Story Spark occurring a bit later, what else does your protagonist want on the first page, and what stands in the way? (This creates the conflict you need to keep reader attention until the Story Spark occurs.)

Odds are in your first draft, you'll start too early, that is, you'll start too long before the Story Spark. Don't worry about it. After you finish the draft and let it sit for a while, it'll be easier to see which part isn't necessary and where the story really becomes compelling. Your beta readers—the first people who read your work after a draft is finished and give you feedback—can also help with this. If any or all feel bored at the beginning, ask at which point the novel really grabbed them.

As you go through these steps to plot your novel, it's okay if you're not yet sure of the exact moment that sparks your story. You can figure out or revise this plot point later once you've filled in the remaining four.

In fact, regardless how sure you are right now, take a fresh look at your Story Spark when you finish all five Points. You may discover a more compelling spark.

Now that you understand the Story Spark, let's talk about the first major plot turn, which comes at the one-quarter point in the novel.

6

THE ONE-QUARTER TWIST

Your novel is rolling along. The protagonist is dealing with the conflict that began with the Story Spark.

Then, a fourth of the way through the story, **something outside of the protagonist raises the stakes and spins the plot in a new direction. Because of it, the protagonist must change course as well.**

This is the **One-Quarter Twist**, and you'll find it about a fourth of the way through in nearly any book you pick up or movie you watch.

As we near the one-quarter point in **Gone With The Wind**, Scarlett, now widowed, is living in Atlanta with Melanie while Ashley is at war.

(The blushing beau who proposed immediately after war was declared was Melanie's brother, Charles, so she and Scarlett are now sisters-in-law.) With Ashley away, Scarlett is free to dream about him, listen to his letters to Melanie being read aloud, and pretend he's coming home to her. The entire city is expecting a Confederate victory and an end to the Civil War.

The One-Quarter Twist happens on pages 177-188 of my hardback copy (page 183.25 is exactly 1/4 through the book). First, the battle at Gettysburg occurs. Many of Scarlett's friends and former suitors are killed. Hope of a Confederate victory is dashed, and though the war is not over, the city will soon be conquered territory. This leaves everyone, including Scarlett, shifting from hope that the Confederacy will soon prevail to coping with loss, death, and eventually what feels like an invading army of Yankees.

Second, Ashley survives the battle and comes home for Christmas. That, at least, makes Scarlett happy—until nighttime comes and she sees Melanie and Ashley go into their bedroom and shut the door. It hits her that she will forever be excluded from this part of Ashley's life. From then on, the story follows Scarlett's personal attempts to survive the War and its aftermath, to care for all the people who come to depend upon her because of it, and to live with her passion for a man she eventually sees nearly every day, but who is married to someone else.

In **The Terminator**, during the first quarter of the movie, Sarah Connor deals with day-to-day conflicts—the challenging restaurant patrons, her roommate's semi-annoying boyfriend, and a cancelled date.

At 25-27 minutes into the 107-minute film—26.75 being the 1/4 mark—the Terminator kills a second woman named Sarah Connor. Our Sarah is out by herself (because of the cancelled date) at a bar and grill. She sees on the news that yet another woman with her name is dead. Earlier in the movie, she saw the newscast about the death of the first Sarah Connor, but she didn't think it affected her. This second murder turns the story and her actions, as she's now afraid for her life.

From the moment Sarah tries to call the police from the broken payphone, her ordinary life is over. The movie becomes the story of her quest to get away from and later to fight the Terminator. This is a perfect One-Quarter Twist, as it completely shifts the story and raises the stakes nearly as high as they can go. For the next quarter of the film, Sarah is reacting to and dealing with this plot turn.

In the first quarter of **The Awakening**, Tara Spencer tells her friends and family that she's pregnant. They don't believe she's never had sex. Her boyfriend breaks up with her, convinced she cheated on him, and her parents are worried about her mental health. At 22,300 words of the 84,900-word book, a religious zealot attacks Tara at her college. This is the first time she realizes there are people who so strongly believe she or her potential child (or both) are evil that they want to kill her. At the same time, her parents try to have her committed to a psychiatric ward.

These events combined cause Tara to change course and accept help from a stranger, Cyril Woods. Until then, Tara was wary of Cyril, a young man from what sounds like a religious cult that believes her pregnancy has save-the-world potential. That scenario makes no sense to Tara, an atheist, and she's certain there must be some scientific or natural explanation. Cyril promises to help her find a safe place to give birth, but in the first quarter of the book Tara has no reason to leave the safety of home. In fact, she has every reason to stay. She's needed at home with her family. Her youngest sister has cancer, and Tara plays a vital role in caring for all her siblings because her parents of necessity are so focused on their ill daughter.

Because of this background, Tara needed a very strong reason to turn to a stranger with a questionable story over her friends and family. It is only because she realizes her life and liberty are at risk that she accepts Cyril's help.

All these examples show not only the plot turn, but how the protagonist lives life before that and copes with difficulties. Sarah Connor gets aggravated at her job, but when she leaves, she puts it behind her. She uses humor when dealing with annoyances, and when her date cancels, she doesn't sit home and mope, she goes out anyway. Scarlett becomes easily angry and works at hiding it, she flirts, she tries to be like the other Southern ladies but violates the rules left and right. She is used to things being done for her—someone to help her dress, to make and set out food for her, to tell her what to say and what to do (even if she often doesn't listen). Tara asks questions about her situation and she's fairly open minded, but she's skeptical and she rejects Cyril's messianic claims.

Think about how your protagonist will deal,

during the first quarter of the book, with the conflict the Story Spark set in motion and with the ordinary conflicts of life.

* **In the first quarter of your novel, what sorts of coping mechanisms would your protagonist use and what actions would the protagonist take?**
* **Now brainstorm dramatic events that could raise the stakes.**
* **How would each event change your protagonist's approach and/or send the protagonist in a new direction?**

If you're not sure about any of the above questions, a great way to spark ideas is to use the **What If** technique. Take out scratch paper or an old notebook—nothing hardbound or fancy looking, as it'll make what you write seem set in stone—and write the words What If on the left margin 20 times. (Use the lines below if you like.) (Use the worksheets if you like.)

* **Off the top of your head, fill in anything you can think of, including big ideas (what if aliens land and wipe out half the Earth's population?), small changes (what if her friend is late for the movie), and everything in between.**

If it works better for you, find an out-of-the-way place and pace or walk or run while you speak What Ifs aloud to yourself.

If you're struggling with the One-Quarter Twist, move on. When you figure out your later points, especially the Mid-Point, the plot twist you need may become clear.

7

THE MID-POINT (NEVER BE HUNGRY AGAIN)

Many writers struggle with the "saggy middle." You know where to start your novel and where to end it, but everything in between feels like filler. The good news is that if you use the 5-Point framework, you'll never need to worry about that problem.

There are lots of ways to approach the halfway point of a novel, and over the decades I've experimented with most of them. Some plot diagrams don't even identify the **Mid-Point**—a sure recipe for a saggy (or soggy) middle. But avoiding that is actually pretty simple.

The protagonist must commit—with a capital C.

The Commitment

Until now, the protagonist has acted mainly in response to the Story Spark and the twist at the one-quarter point, often feeling knocked about by fierce winds. Think about Sarah Connor struggling to get through to the police, fleeing the Terminator, and taking refuge in a police station. She is literally on the run. She is reacting more than acting.

At the Mid-Point all that changes. The protagonist throws in her whole heart, throws caution to the wind, and **commits to pursuing the quest, fighting for what's right, or doing whatever is needed to reach the desired end.**

The classic example comes from **Gone With The Wind.** After the war, Scarlett returns to her home, longing for comfort from her mother and the chance to lay down the burdens she's been carrying. At home, though, she finds her mother dead, her father half-senile, and her sisters in denial or deathly ill. There is literally no food. Every question Scarlett asks about possible food is a dead end. She goes to the neighbor's vegetable garden, finds some old vegetables, eats them, and vomits.

Lying on the ground, desperate, starving, and frightened, she rises up and vows, with God as her witness, she will never be hungry again.

That is the Mid-Point of the book and movie. It drives the rest of the story. Every action listed below that Scarlett takes arises from her vow:

- Marries her sister's only boyfriend, Frank Kennedy, because he owns a store and its income can be used to support her family and their plantation;
- Shoves Frank aside when she realizes she can run the store better than he can;
- Flouts convention by buying and running sawmills;
- Travels alone despite being a woman and later being (gasp!) pregnant;
- Marries Rhett Butler for his money;
- And on and on....

She Will Never Be Hungry Again. No saggy middle there.

The Mid-Point can also be a point of Reversal, where everything changes and the protagonist realizes this is For Real.

The Terminator includes both a Reversal and the main character committing. For the first half of the movie, Sarah is still operating from her ordinary-world perspective. When she discovers she's being stalked, she flees, and she accepts help from the police. She believes their explanation that Reese, who claims he's there to help her fight a cyborg from the future, is crazy. She accepts that her attacker is really a human hyped up on drugs and wearing a bulletproof vest.

The Reversal happens when the Terminator crashes into the police station, killing everyone, seemingly unstoppable. Sarah comes to believe what the audience already knew—we are not in the ordinary world, and the Terminator is not human. Sarah commits when she chooses to believe Reese's tale of the future. She emerges from her hiding place in the police station and flees with him. (That she now believes everything Reese told her is shown in the next major scene where the two hide outside overnight.) Her life will never be the same again. Once again, no saggy middle here.

In **The Awakening**, there's also a Reversal followed by a Commitment. During the first half of the book, Tara feels threatened, and she's injured in the knife attack by the zealot at the One-Quarter Twist. But she's still alive, and everyone around her is safe. At the Mid-Point, though, a bomb meant for Tara kills one of her allies. That's the Reversal. Determined that no one else will die because of her, she throws caution to the wind. Telling no one where she's going, she leaves all her friends and allies and commits to seeking answers alone with nothing but a fake ID, some borrowed clothes and a wig to help disguise herself, and a small amount of cash.

For more examples of Mid-Points, check the page count of one of your favorite books or the running time of your favorite movie and see what happens halfway through. I'm betting you'll see a Reversal and/or the protagonist doing the equivalent of vowing to never be hungry again. (When I was first learning the 5-Point plot structure, I checked my watch frequently in movies. Which shows you how long I've been using this structure, as I haven't worn a watch since smartphones were invented.)

The Mid-Point is also a great place to do the What If exercise. Play out the different ideas in your mind to see which one creates a Reversal, causes the main character to make a vow and commit, or both.

Think about what could happen at the halfway point in your novel that would reverse the protagonist's fortunes, alter the world, or set up a completely new dynamic.

* **List some What Ifs.**

* Choose one or two and describe it in more detail.

Now consider what your protagonist can commit to that will address the major conflict.

* Write a few more What Ifs on this if it helps you sort through your ideas.
* Which of the What Ifs you wrote strikes you as most compelling?
* Why?
* How would your protagonist finish the sentence "As God is my witness, I will...."
* Once your protagonist commits, how will that change her/his/its choices and actions from then on?

If you're uncertain, as before, keep moving. The Mid-Point drives the rest of the story. If you figure out the last two points, what your protagonist needs to vow at the Mid-Point and/or what type of Reversal will work best will be clear.

8

THE THREE-QUARTER TURN

The next major plot turn after your Mid-Point occurs about three-quarters through your novel. It takes the story in a new and often unexpected direction, as did the twist at the one-quarter point. **Unlike the One-Quarter Twist, though, which comes from outside the protagonist, the Three-Quarter Turn arises directly from the protagonist's choice at the Mid-Point.** This ensures your main character takes action throughout the second half of the novel, rather than merely being carried along by events outside her or his control.

In **Gone With The Wind**, as Scarlett drives her carriage home from her sawmill, two men (one

Black and one white) attack her. The attack arises from the Mid-Point because, as we saw above, Scarlett's vow means she continues to do things the people of Atlanta view as appalling in order to make money, including running the sawmill and driving alone. She isn't physically hurt, but she is frightened and upset.

Unknown to Scarlett, her husband Frank Kennedy and the other men in her circle (including her beloved Ashley) belong to the Ku Klux Klan. They go on a raid to "avenge" Scarlett's attack. Frank Kennedy is killed and Ashley is wounded. Rhett Butler covers for the men with the local authorities. Rhett also proposes to Scarlett, and she accepts, before Frank's body is cold. In this way, the attack at the three-quarter point drives the rest of the story.

The Old Guard of Southern Society blames Scarlett for the Klan's raid and the loss of their men, making her even more of a pariah. Her choice to marry Rhett further scandalizes everyone, despite that he's earned a lot of points by protecting the men. Scarlett's position in society also changes because now she has all the money she wants and she spends lavishly, alienating those who live in genteel poverty. Her relationship with

Ashley becomes more complicated. As significant, Scarlett has a daughter with Rhett, and her death and Scarlett's miscarriage during a second pregnancy lead directly into the book's climax.

Note that the attack on Scarlett happens on page 558 of the 733-page novel. Page 549.75 is the 3/4 point. Did Margaret Mitchell deliberately plan that? I've no idea, but I'm sure she had a sense that there needed to be a major turn in a story that already was epic in scope.

The Three-Quarter Turn is sometimes a combination of events. In **The Terminator**, at 82 minutes into the 107-minute movie (81 being the 3/4 mark), Sarah's decision to flee and fight with Kyle Reese leads to her and Kyle making love and conceiving John Connor (though we don't know that yet), who will grow up to fight Skynet. In the scene right before that, Sarah called her mother, who presumably saw news coverage of the bloodbath at the police station, to tell her she's safe. That results in the Terminator tracking Kyle and Sarah to the motel. This happens minutes after the exact three-quarter point in the movie. Sarah spends the rest of the film fighting the Terminator to the death.

In **The Awakening**, Tara's travels, which she undertook at the Mid-Point, lead her to a community run by an Armenian woman whose daughter was killed decades before while pregnant. That young woman, too, was a pregnant virgin. This information prompts Tara to travel to Armenia with Cyril Woods. His research suggests she'll find answers there and perhaps holy ground where she can safely give birth.

Though the religious order Cyril belongs to sees Tara as an imposter because her child will be female, Cyril believes in her and has fallen for her. At the three-quarter point, the two make love (you can see **The Terminator** influence here). This event turns the story because in the morning, Cyril accuses Tara of seducing him and abandons her in Armenia. When Tara explores on her own, she can't find the site Cyril spoke of, but she does connect with relatives of the Armenian pregnant virgin. Based on a vision she has after working with them, she reveals to the world her virgin pregnancy claim, which drives the events that follow.

If you don't know your Three-Quarter Turn right now, but you do know your Climax scene—the scene that resolves the story conflict—think about what event or choice will best propel the story toward that resolution. Remember, as always, you're not trying to make things easy on the protagonist. In fact, asking yourself what is the worst thing that can happen at this moment to the protagonist is not a bad way to generate this plot point.

You can also use the What If exercise, keeping in mind what your protagonist did or chose at the Mid-Point. If you haven't figured out your Mid-Point yet, brainstorm some turns at the three-quarter point that would require a vow, commitment, or life-changing action by the protagonist at the Mid-Point.

* What is the worst thing that could happen to your protagonist right now? (Write down at least 5 options.)
* How does each of these possible turns grow out of the protagonist's choice or action at the Mid-Point?
* How does each lead to a Climax (the point where your main conflict resolves)
* Which of these do you think works best as your Three-Quarter Turn?
* If none of your "worst thing" options seems right, brainstorm other dramatic three-quarter turns.
* How does each of these possible turns grow out of the protagonist's choice or action at the Mid-Point?

* How does each lead to a Climax (the point where your main conflict resolves)

You can choose one of your options now as your novel's Three-Quarter Turn or hold off and decide when we're finished. Because you're almost done....

9

THE CLIMAX

This is it. The big payoff. One way or another, the central conflict of the book ends. The protagonist may out-and-out win, may be defeated utterly, may win partially (often seen in series books), or may win but at such a cost it leaves him or her devastated (known as a pyrrhic victory).

The Climax is the scene your reader is most likely to remember, for good or for ill. However you end the conflict, it must end.

In **Gone With The Wind**, Scarlett confesses her love for Rhett, which she only became aware of recently herself. But it's too late. Her seeming indifference even as she suffered through her miscarriage and her pursuit of Ashley eroded Rhett's feelings, and he says what's broken can't be repaired. Scarlett's standing in the community has also been ruined. Ironically, Melanie was her one defender, and with her death Scarlett has nothing. This is the out-and-out loss, though there is a bit of hope, which we'll discuss when we talk about Falling Action in Chapter Twelve.

In **The Awakening**, Tara's openness about her virgin pregnancy leads to a threat to her brother's life. With him in jeopardy, Tara is forced to give a press conference to recant her claim to a supernatural pregnancy. Her willingness to cast herself in a bad light to save someone she loves creates the sacred place she needs to give birth. She goes into labor and gives birth at the foot of the St. Louis Arch on national television. Her mother and father are there with her, supporting her, showing the rift between them and Tara has healed.

This Climax is a partial win, as it resolves the main story question of whether Tara will be able to survive and deliver her child safely into the world. It also resolves the conflict with her parents, who have accepted that Tara told the truth about having no idea how she'd become pregnant. Because **The Awakening** is the first in a series, it leaves open the questions of Tara's and her child's roles in the world and in the battle of good and evil.

In **The Terminator**, Kyle Reese is dead, Sarah Connor has a broken leg, and the Terminator, though missing the lower half of its body, pursues her relentlessly through a factory. She traps the Terminator in a conveyor belt, but it reaches through bars and wraps its hand around her throat. She hits a button so the machinery crushes the Terminator. This could be seen as a pyrrhic victory, as Sarah has lost Reese and her ordinary world forever. But it can also be seen as an out-an-out win, as she survived the ordeal and may still be able to help humanity avert the coming crisis.

Not only do you want to resolve the conflict in a satisfying way, **you want the scene itself to be dramatic.** Rhett and Scarlett fight in the dining room of the garish mansion Rhett built for her—a symbol of their married life as well as of Scarlett's penchant for provoking the impoverished, genteel Southerners in her circle with her wealth and success. Sarah fights the Terminator in a factory full of pipes, metal, gears, and whirling, clanking machine parts. It provides a perfect setting for the chasing and fighting, as well as a fitting end for the cyborg. Tara gives her press conference at noon under the St. Louis Arch when an eclipse is expected. The eclipse happens a few minutes early, plunging the world into darkness as she goes into labor.

Think about your Climax.

* **What location would provide a dramatic backdrop for the events?**
* **Who is there?**
* **How did you resolve your major conflict? Did the protagonist achieve the goal?**
* **If your protagonist won, what was the cost?**
* **What happened to the antagonist?**

Congratulations! You've finished the most challenging parts of plotting your novel. It's downhill from here. But first....

10
TAKING A BREAK

You created your plot points, so it's time to take a break. (You didn't know you got breaks, did you?) You not only deserve one, it's vital to take one. It will give your mind a rest, allowing you to return to your story with fresh eyes.

So set your five plot points aside for a few days or, even better, a week. When you come back, see how they fit together.

Now ask yourself these questions:

- Does your Story Spark ignite enough conflict?
- Does your One-Quarter Twist come

from outside the protagonist and truly spin the story in a new direction?
- Does your protagonist throw caution to the wind at the Mid-Point and/or is there a Reversal?
- Does the Mid-Point drive the story forward?
- Does your Three-Quarter Turn flow from the Mid-Point and shift the story once more in a new direction?
- Does your Three-Quarter Turn lead directly to the Climax?
- Do you resolve your major plot at the Climax?
- Do you answer the story questions your reader needs answered?

If you answered no to any of the above, revisit the appropriate sections and revise.

Once you're satisfied with your five points, it's time to talk about subplots.

11

STEP THREE: SUBPLOTS

Most, though not all, novels have a subplot and possibly more than one. Subplots are secondary storylines that are usually less complex than the main plot (also known as the A Plot). They affect the A Plot, sometimes significantly, sometimes in a minor way, and they get less screen time, so to speak, than the central conflict but are still important.

A subplot may involve your protagonist and intersect with the A Plot, such as where the protagonist falls in love or works through a personal issue as well as pursuing the separate goal that drives the action. In **The Terminator**, for example, the relationship between Kyle Reese and Sarah Connor is its own subplot, with Reese as the viewpoint character. He literally travels across time for Sarah and dies for her. That subplot intersects at the Mid-Point with the A plot, as Sarah and Reese making love influences the rest of the story for both the main plot and subplot. It also suggests a possible victory over not only the Terminator, but Skynet.

Other subplots don't feature the main character at all but involve side characters with their own storylines that intersect with or support the A Plot. The relationship of Melanie and Ashley in **Gone With The Wind** is a good example of that, as is the relationship between Scarlett and Melanie.

Throughout the book (and film), Ashley seems to have great affection for Melanie but also to be in love with Scarlett. In many ways he leads Scarlett on, confessing how drawn he is to her and embracing her even as rejects her. Melanie believes the best of everyone she loves and doesn't see any of the attraction between her husband and sister-in-law. She is steady and kind and also courageous and determined, and eventually the jealous Scarlett comes to see Melanie's good qualities and rely upon her. Ashley finally realizes what he feels for Melanie is deep love and what he feels for Scarlett is physical attraction, though he also likes and admires Scarlett. Both Scarlett and Ashley truly appreciate their love for Melanie when she dies shortly before the end of the book.

This resolution isn't completely necessary for the A Plot between Rhett and Scarlett, as Scarlett has already begun to discover she loves Rhett, but it contributes. It also affects Scarlett's conflict with the South's Old Guard, as Melanie was her one defender. So it contributes to and deepens the A Plot conflicts.

Still other subplots involve side characters but are necessary to the main story arc. In **Terminator 2**, a subplot is John Connor's need for a father and growing love for the Terminator. This makes the moment when the Terminator sacrifices himself heart-wrenching. This subplot is one reason it's easy to shift a bit and see John as the protagonist. For the reasons I talked about in Chapter Two, though, The Terminator plays that role.

Your subplot also may involve the antagonist. In **The Awakening**, one subplot is Cyril Woods' struggle with his religious beliefs. In the beginning, he is devoted to the Brotherhood of Andrew and does everything he's told to do. He's a former soldier, and his mentor in the Brotherhood helped him through an extremely difficult time in his life. Knowing and beginning to love Tara challenges his devotion when the Brotherhood turns on her. Around the three-quarter point in the A Plot, he throws caution to the wind by making love with Tara. But his guilt is intense. He feels he's betrayed everything he's supposed to believe in. In turmoil, he blames Tara and throws himself into the Brotherhood with new fervor, committing crimes on its behalf in an attempt to atone.

Despite his conflicts, or maybe because of them, Cyril is one of my favorite characters, and I've heard the same from readers. Though his beliefs change radically, each and every time he tries to do what he sincerely believes is right. Readers both hate him and hope for his redemption.

For a subplot that does not directly involve the protagonist, in **The Unbelievers**, the second book in my **Awakening** series, Tara's dad and Cyril Woods team up to search for a piece of a prophecy about Tara. The search is necessary to the A Plot because the prophecy matters. The subplot itself, though, is how Pete Spencer (Tara's dad) deals with the challenge Tara's supernatural pregnancy presents to his traditional religious views, and the ways he feels he's failed her because he's been so rigid. Pete projects onto Cyril his own failings. Through getting to know and working with Cyril,

Pete finally comes to terms with his traditional beliefs and his love for his daughter.

Now that your A Plot is in good order, think about potential subplots. As you brainstorm, ask yourself these questions:

- What character or characters other than your protagonist and antagonist most interest you?
- What obstacles might those characters face in seeking their personal goals?
- What sorts of conflicts exist in those characters' personal relationships?
- What other conflicts could exist for your protagonist that would make life harder?
- What other conflicts could exist for your antagonist that would make life harder?

*This is another great place to use the What If exercise. List some What Ifs about your characters that go beyond the central conflict.

You can plan your subplots using the same five points in the same order. The difference is that where those points occur within your novel will depend less on how far into the novel you are—

that is, whether you are a quarter way through, halfway through, etc.—and more on how the subplot fits with your main story. That means you'll have a Story Spark, but it may not occur until a third of the way into the book. There should be a first twist, but it may be earlier or later than the one-quarter point of the novel. Those points may also be subtler and less dramatic than the ones in your A Plot. Your subplot may resolve before the Climax, at the same time, or after it.

Because of this flexibility, I often weave in the subplot when there is a natural lull in the main plot. That way the reader gets a sense of time passing and is engaged in the meantime by a separate storyline.

I also use the subplot to illuminate parts of the A plot. In **The Awakening**, the conflict between Tara and her parents is a subplot. They've always had her back before, but they turn on her when she insists she's pregnant and doesn't know how it happened. They aren't trying to be malicious. They're acting out of worry for her. That worry causes them to try to have Tara committed to a psychiatric ward and drives her away at the one-quarter point of the A plot. In that way, Tara's parents serve as a stand in for what most people, and so most readers, would think about a young woman who asserts a virgin pregnancy—that she's lying to get attention, is in denial, or is mentally unwell and needs help. It underscores how isolated and lost Tara feels.

While it can be helpful to figure out the five points for your subplots, winging it is also a workable option. That's because so long as your A Plot is in good shape, you can comfortably experiment with your subplot(s) without needing to revamp your entire book.

*Take a few minutes to write down potential five points for one or more of your subplots now.

Now we'll get to the last planning step for your novel, the Falling Action. It'll only take a few minutes, because you've laid the groundwork. (You have, right? If not, that's okay, go ahead and read the rest anyway.)

12

STEP FOUR: FALLING ACTION

You have your central conflict, other less significant conflicts, and your main characters with strong opposing goals. You've plotted your five points, including the Climax, which resolves that central conflict. So you're ready for Step Four, sketching our your Falling Action.

Everything after the Climax of your main plot is **the Falling Action.** This is where you tie up loose ends, answer questions you've left open that you feel your reader will need resolved, hint at the future, and finish any subplots that are hanging out there.

If you're planning a sequel, or you want to leave a bit to the reader's imagination, you can leave a few questions open. Too many, though, and your story won't stand alone. That is not always a bad thing. **The Empire Strikes Back** ended on a cliffhanger and many viewers see it as the best of the original Star Wars trilogy. Be ready for complaints from readers, however.

In **Gone With The Wind**, the Falling Action takes less than a page. Devastated, Scarlett resolves to return home to the plantation to heal and figure out how to get Rhett back. It's left to the reader to decide whether that's possible. Scarlett thinks there's hope, as she ends with her trademark "tomorrow is another day."

The Falling Action in **The Awakening** is a little more than a page. After safely giving birth, Tara realizes both her little brother and Cyril have been wounded, perhaps fatally. Her parents, who are at her side, take the newborn. Tara discovers she's developed the power to heal, and she revives her brother after he appears to have died at the hand of Cyril Woods. (Cyril had a needle filled with poison at her brother's throat at the start of the press conference.) Cyril, whom Tara heals of a bullet wound, regrets all he's done to hurt Tara and allows the police to lead him away. Still open, however, are the roles Tara and her child will play in the world and in the battle between good and evil. Those questions take three more books to resolve.

Some readers in reviews were upset that there wasn't a definitive answer to the meaning of Tara's supernatural pregnancy. The second book, **The Unbelievers**, also didn't answer that question, as there were two books left in the series. Book 2 resolved its main story arc regarding the ancient prophecy, as well as the subplot about Tara's dad. But the prophecy led to further questions, and the scenes in the Falling Action set the conflict for the next book. Readers who like serialized stories enjoyed that, but others were unhappy and may have stopped reading the series.

The Terminator strikes an excellent balance of being complete in itself and leaving story questions open for a potential sequel. Sarah defeats the Terminator, a satisfying conclusion to the central conflict. At the film's end, we see Sarah driving out of the country and recording messages to her unborn child. This is the first time we learn that she got pregnant when she and Kyle Reese had sex. If we'd ended with her crushing the Terminator, we might have guessed at that development, but we wouldn't have known for sure. Still, many questions remain. The Terminator's arm survives and is preserved. Kyle Reese told Sarah the future is not set, so it's not certain that her child will, in fact, grow up to lead a rebellion. And, finally, nuclear war is still on the horizon and may or may not be avoidable. And so, despite a finished film, a franchise was born. (My favorite follow up was the television series **The Sarah Connor Chronicles.**)

Your Falling Action

Now that you've plotted your five points, including your Climax, and considered your subplots, think about what your reader needs to know and what questions you feel are best left to the imagination.

* **What questions did your story raise that weren't resolved?**
* **Which ones are you comfortable leaving to the reader's imagination? (Or leaving for a sequel?)**
* **How will you resolve the rest?**

Give yourself a hand—you're finished planning! Take time to celebrate. Take a few minutes for a cup of your favorite tea, read for a half hour, spend an afternoon walking in the prettiest place you can find, or do something else you enjoy.

When you come back, we'll talk about point of view.

13

STEP FIVE: WHOSE STORY IS IT?

Your protagonist and antagonist are motivated and have mutually-exclusive goals. Your plot points are in good shape. That means you're ready to write—almost.

Why almost? Because you need to decide **who will tell your story.**

The two main guidelines when deciding from whose point of view to tell your entire novel or a particular scene are as follows:

> Use the overall point of view that works best for your story.

> A scene is strongest when told by the character with the most to lose.

Before we figure out which point of view works best, a quick overview of your point-of-view options:

- Third person omniscient
- Third person limited shifting (multiple characters)
- Third person limited (single character)
- Second person
- First person

You probably remember the differences between third, second, and first person from your high school literature class. **Third person POV** uses the pronouns "she" or "he" rather than "you" or "I" when telling the story:

> John rushed into the room, afraid he'd make a poor first impression by being late.

Second person POV, which is rarely used in fiction, uses the pronoun "you," as if you were writing about the reader as a character in the novel:

> You rushed into the room, afraid you'd make a poor first impression by being late.

First person POV uses the pronoun "I":

I rushed into the room, afraid I'd make a poor first impression by being late.

To decide which works best, let's talk about the pluses and minuses of each. I'll start with first person because the mechanics of it are the simplest, though it's not necessarily the easiest to write.

First Person

One drawback of first person is that your novel can't include anything that the viewpoint character/narrator doesn't know. If you're writing from the point of view of your protagonist and she or he doesn't know there's a bomb underneath the table, you can't tell the reader the bomb is there.

You also can't directly state what any other character is thinking or feeling. The reader only knows what the other characters say or do as seen through the narrator's eyes. Your narrator can guess—or your reader can guess—based on the other characters' actions, facial expressions, or body language, but that's all.

So why use first person narration? It adds a greater sense of immediacy, and the reader is likely to connect and identify more with the viewpoint character. It also allows you as the writer to explore more deeply the narrator's life, feelings, thoughts, background, and motivation.

Also, it's simpler. There are fewer decisions to make. You know from whose point of view each scene will be told from page one. You also know exactly what you can and can't share with the reader.

Finally, first person narration reads the way the character would speak if telling the story to a friend. That can be a plus or a minus. On the one hand, you'll need to work harder at developing a unique voice for your narrator. On the other, it may be easier and more fun to do that, as you'll be so immersed in the narrator's viewpoint.

If your readers love the character's voice, they will buy book after book. One of my favorite fictional characters is V.I. Warshawski. The books are told in the first person, and I buy every one as soon as Sara Paretsky releases it. V.I. is a great example if you want to read a strong first person narrative.

Second Person

Second person provides the same pluses and minuses as first person. That's so because it is basically first person but substituting "you" for "I" and "me."

There are some added facets, which I'll get to.

But first, because it's fairly rare in fiction, I suggest you get on line (or visit a library or bookstore) and read the opening pages of **Bright Lights Big City** for a good example of second person.

Here are the first few sentences. The author uses not only second person but present tense, which creates a greater urgency:

> You are not the kind of guy who would be at a place like this at this time of the morning. But here you are, and you cannot say that the train is entirely unfamiliar, although the details are fuzzy. You are at a nightclub talking to a girl with a shaved head.

The use of "you" makes the reader feel even closer to the main character. The reader is plunged right into the scene. Second person also tends to make a writer less inclined to ramble on about backstory or engage in unnecessary flashbacks. Something about writing as if you're talking about the reader inhibits that, because if you were actually writing about the reader, the reader would already know her or his background.

An added disadvantage of second person over first person is that it is uncommon enough that it may initially be distracting to the reader. If it is a type of writing that seems compelling to you, though, give it a try. Most readers forget about the "you" after a few lines.

Third Person

The third person approach is the most complex because it allows for three variations that affect on a scene-by-scene level how you'll tell your story.

Third person limited (single character) is the easiest to manage. "Single character" means just that. As in first and second person, the same character tells the entire story. The difference is that rather than "I" or "you," you'll use "he" or "she" (or perhaps "it") when referring to the viewpoint character.

The "limited" aspect once again refers to knowing only what that the viewpoint character knows. So, as in first and second person, even if you as the author know there's a bomb under the table, you can't tell the reader about it unless or until the viewpoint character knows it.

Likewise, your viewpoint character can't see into the head or hearts of other characters.

As with first and second person, this type of narration can delve deep into the viewpoint character's mind and heart. The feel may be a bit more removed because "I" and "you" are out of the picture, other than in dialogue. The narration also is less conversational than first person, though it can still give a feel for the character's voice.

Whether you use first person or third person limited, single character, mostly depends on what you enjoy reading or writing more. It also may depend on the market. Trends come and go, and if a book becomes popular that's first person, you'll suddenly see lots more first person books out there.

Certain genres, too, are more apt to use first person than others. Private eye novels (including the V.I. Warshawki novels I mentioned) are often first person. It gives the reader a strong sense of solving the mystery with the sleuth. But there are no hard and fast rules, so write whatever you enjoy the most.

Third person limited shifting (multiple character) means that you tell the story from the viewpoints of more than one character. But you still are limited to sharing what is known and experienced by the viewpoint character when you are in that character's mind. The shifts from one character's point of view to another's occur either at scene breaks or chapter breaks.

Also, while you can shift from one character's

POV to another's, you can't include a fact that none of your viewpoint characters knows.

Exception: Once in a while, an author breaks out of the limited viewpoint to share a generally-known fact for background. For instance, my standalone supernatural suspense novel **When Darkness Falls** is mainly set in downtown Chicago, and my two viewpoint characters are in their mid-twenties. In that novel, if it's important to the story, I could include a detail about the Chicago L trains without making clear which viewpoint character knows the information, or that any character knows it. Such background information usually comes at the beginning or end of a chapter or scene.

If you need to do this, the key is to make sure it's not distracting to the reader. In my example, if in description I mention that the Red Line runs north and south, the reader probably won't wonder which character's point of view that comes from. But if I give a long history of the first L train, and talk about how each line used to be known only by destination and not color, the reader will likely start wondering whether my two twenty-something viewpoint characters actually know that and why.

You'll see third person limited shifting most

often in thrillers. It gives the reader the chance to see the story unfold from different perspectives and allows tension to build when the reader knows something that the viewpoint character doesn't. If the antagonist is a viewpoint character and knows there's a bomb under the table but the protagonist doesn't, the reader worries for the protagonist. That ratchets up tension.

Third person omniscient is the broadest and most flexible approach, but it can be the most challenging to write.

It's **omniscient** because the narrator can see into everyone's mind. Not only that, the narrator can go beyond the experiences and knowledge of the characters. For example, the story could start with a history of a town, a company, or a country regardless whether any of the main characters know that history. A scene could begin with a bird's eye view of a city block and gradually zero in on a single seat on a single train car. Think of first scenes in movies that give you a wide shot of a town, then zoom in on a street, then a house, then a person walking out of a house. That's the equivalent of the omniscient narrator.

The omniscient narrator also can opine about the character from a step back, rather than being locked into a character's perspective.

The first two lines of **Gone With The Wind** provide an example of omniscient narration:

> Scarlett O'Hara was not beautiful, but men seldom realized it when caught by her charm as the Tarleton twins were. In her face were too sharply blended the delicate features of her mother, a Coast aristocrat of French descent, and the heavy ones of her florid Irish father.

In these sentences, we are in neither Scarlett's nor the twins' POVs. Rather, we get a big picture view of Scarlett. Scarlett herself, for instance, would be unlikely to describe herself as "not beautiful," and the Tarleton twins probably wouldn't describe her that way or refer to her mother's and father's ancestry if asked to tell someone what she looked like.

Later in the chapter the story zooms in so that we get Scarlett's internal thoughts and feelings as well as those of the Tarletons, but there are many passages in the book that provide a sweeping view of Southern society, the war, and politics. Those are all told via the omniscient narrator.

The pluses of omniscient narration are the big picture scope and feel, as well as the flexibility. As a writer, you can swoop into the viewpoint of whatever character you choose, and you can back off and give the perspective of many people at once. Omniscient is the perfect choice for **Gone With The Wind** because Margaret Mitchell is able to provide numerous perspectives when she needs to, including soldiers on the front lines, prisoners of war, society matrons, or carpetbaggers. She can also include descriptions of lands and cultures and characters that are rich with history and details that no one particular character is aware of.

The disadvantages include that writing in omniscient narration can be unwieldy. As the author, you have so many choices for every single scene that it can be overwhelming. Also, a lot of care is needed to avoid jarring the reader when you head hop from one character to another or zoom in or out from a bird's eye view to a single character's view. You can avoid this to some extent by only switching POV from scene to scene or chapter to chapter, but then you may as well use third person limited shifting. Another method is to use a character's line of dialogue or a movement by the character to segue into that character's perspective.

In addition, because of the big picture perspective, your reader may not feel as connected to or invested in any particular character. Partly for this reason, omniscient narration, which is common in many classics, is not often used today in fiction. Most readers want to feel as if they are truly seeing through the eyes of, or living in the body of, one or more characters, and it's hard to feel that way with omniscient narration. Today's readers also are unused to shifts of point of view within scenes, and it may distract them or make them wonder if you shifted deliberately or made an error.

You see omniscient narration used more in literary novels than in popular or genre fiction. Literary books focus more on the writing itself than the plot (though how much more varies) and also tend to leave more for the reader to infer about the characters' thoughts and feelings. This makes such books better suited to an omniscient narrator, as readers don't have the same expectation of closeness with the viewpoint characters, and they expect to work harder to understand the story.

In short, because they may be unfamiliar with omniscient narration, some readers may be thrown off by it. If you are writing an epic or sweeping tale, though, or you simply love the approach, give it a try.

One More Variation

Some books shift scene-to-scene or chapter-to-chapter from first person told by one character to third person limited told by another character. You might do this if you have a very strong sense of one character's voice and you really want to write using "I," but third person seems more appropriate for one or more other viewpoint characters.

You can also shift from one first person viewpoint to another first person viewpoint. This can be a bit trickier, as the reader is more apt to be confused and assume the same "I" is speaking. While you can certainly put a character name on the top of a chapter or scene to signal the switch to the reader, beware: not all readers look at those tags. I tend to overlook them myself, just as I rarely read chapter titles.

To truly do shifting first person right, the changing voice of the current narrator alone ought to cue the reader. That can be quite challenging. But you can make it work if you're willing to really listen to how each character speaks and make the effort to get that down on the page.

The popular thriller **Gone Girl** is an excellent example of an author using two different first-person narratives—a husband's and a wife's. Both the viewpoint character's voices and the actual story change dramatically depending upon which POV we're in.

In the more recent thriller **Right Behind You**, Lisa Gardner shifts between two first-person points of view—a teenaged girl and her estranged older brother—and two third-person points of view—profilers Quincy and Rainie, who are foster parents to the girl.

Which POV Is "Right"

When choosing from the above point-of-view options, ask yourself what your reader needs to know and when. Answering that question will go the farthest toward whether you write your novel from one character's point of view, whether you shift between characters, or whether you need an omniscient narrator. After that, in a big picture sense, it's what point of view you enjoy writing. For example, if you love first-person narratives and that will work for your story, try it out. If you've always wanted to experiment with omniscient, do that.

But don't spend too long trying to decide before you start writing. Just pick one and go. Why? Because if you start in one POV and discover you need to use another, you can switch in your next scene or chapter and see how that works. There's no need to go back and revise the earlier sections—just make a note to yourself to reconsider point of view on your rewrite. If there are elements you want to include in a scene or chapter you've written (another character's thoughts, a fact the current viewpoint character doesn't know), write that down, too, so you won't forget it when you revise and wonder why you thought you should change POVs.

What's At Stake

Now to the second rule—choosing the character with the most at stake. If you're using a shifting point of view, narrating each scene from the standpoint of the character with the most to lose is the best way to keep the reader engaged. This goes along with what we talked about in Chapter Two when I said the protagonist must care. So, too, your viewpoint character must care.

Under this approach, if you are writing a break up scene, think about who is most invested in the relationship and who will be most devastated if it's over. That character is probably the one whose viewpoint will jump off the page. On the other hand, if for the character choosing to end the relationship, the worst thing in the world is to hurt someone else, that might be the viewpoint character to use.

At a story level, if you're choosing a single character as your viewpoint character, who has the most at stake often is the right choice. But your reader might need a wider perspective or the view of someone one step removed.

A great example of first person narration by someone other than the protagonist is **The Great Gatsby**. Nick, our narrator, is Gatsby's neighbor. Because he's a step (or a plot of land) away, he can show us how Gatsby fits into the society around him in a way that Gatsby himself couldn't. He can also tell us about things that happen that are unknown to Gatsby but that impact him.

Again, experiment. I often switch the point of view of a scene when I rewrite to see if it works better. The key is to save your first draft so you can easily restore the scene if you don't like the change.

14

WRITING FROM POINT TO POINT

Now you know who is telling your story, or at least you have enough of an idea to start writing. You have your main characters and your plot points. That means you're ready to write from one plot point to the next until you finish your first draft.

> **Remember: Your goal in writing your first draft is to write as much as you can as fast as you can, <u>not</u> to write a perfect draft or the best draft you can write.**

This is vital. There are two reasons you need to get to the end of your novel before making major revisions. First, if you rewrite as you go, it's more likely you won't ever complete the novel. I know writers who've rewritten the first third of one novel for years. No one wants to read a third of a novel.

Second, if you rewrite as you go, you'll waste a lot of time. A lot. That's because you can't truly tell what needs to be fixed or improved in the first half of your book until the last half is done. **Sometimes a scene doesn't work because you don't need it, and you won't know that until your novel is complete.** There's nothing more frustrating than rewriting a scene ten times to get it "right," or perhaps simply adequate, only to realize when you finish the book that you don't need that scene.

To get started, look at your notes on your conflict, your protagonist, and your antagonist. Start your first scene (and chapter) with whatever absolutely needs to happen to set the stage and lead into the Story Spark. Don't worry if you feel like you might be starting too early or too late in the narrative. You can always cut, add, or rearrange later.

Once you've written your first scene, either write your Story Spark scene, or write the next scene you need to get there. Add another scene and another, if you need to, but remember, your Spark should happen early.

Once you're written your Story Spark, fill in

the scenes you need to get to the One-Quarter Twist. Keep going the same way from point to point.

Tips On Getting That First Draft Done:

- If the points don't hit at exactly the right spot in the manuscript, keep moving. You can rearrange later so that they do, which will keep your pacing strong;
- If you know something needs to happen to get where you're going but you're stuck on how it should happen or who will be involved, make a note in brackets about what should happen, boldface the note, and move on to the next scene;
- If you need more information to finish a scene or make it realistic, note that in brackets, boldface the note, finish the scene, and fill it in later (are you seeing a theme?);
- If you aren't sure on point of view, rather than wrack your brain, pick one and make a note about other possible points of view in boldface and brackets and move on.

I use this technique all the time. Below are the notes from the first draft of Chapters 1 and 2 of **The Unbelievers:**

[explain why he didn't follow them – also does this fit time frame?]
 [animals?] lived in the trees and brush, but Tara knew their sound, and this wasn't it.
 A plastic bowl half-filled with strained peaches [she's too young for this? Does Tara breastfeed?], spoon propped in it, sat on the kitchenette table.
 Six months [check] before, when Tara had been pregnant
 After seven days of unprecedented rainfall in Thailand, monks at the southern edge of Bangkok [check geography & number of days] crowd into cramped spaces to perform chants

I left all those notes just as you see them in my first draft. When I finished it, I hit Ctrl-F in Word and searched for [. If the missing information was easy to find and fill in, I did quick research and made the appropriate changes. Similarly, if there were simple changes to make—I forgot a character's name when I was writing and now I remembered it—I filled that in, too.

On more complex questions, I left the notes to consider when I read the first draft on paper. Why? Because if I decided to cut the whole scene, or the particular line dropped out, I wouldn't need to fill in the blanks.

That saved me a lot of time.

What If You're Really Stuck?

If you hit a major snag, and you find none of your scenes feels right or makes sense, revisit your conflict, your main characters, and your plot points. You may need to rework them. If so, once you've changed your characters or their goals or revised your plot points (or done all three), I still advise simply making a bracketed note wherever you're at in the manuscript about what you'll change in the preceding pages. After that, keep writing from that point on just as if you'd already made the changes.

A note like that about two-thirds through the manuscript might read: **[change POV to Mary's, make 1/4 Twist her mom's death, not the incident at work]**. You can make the actual revisions immediately after you finish the first draft and before you print it or when you do your first major revision.

Are you getting the idea that I believe in finishing at all costs?

That's because you can and should revise your entire manuscript at least twice before you call your novel finished. So don't stress over making each scene perfect or worry about whether you're including too many or too few scenes.

For now, the important thing is to get the first draft down. So have fun, get to know your characters, and keep writing from one point to the next.

Rewriting Your Novel

Once you finish your draft, print it out and let it sit for two weeks or a month. This will give you the distance you need to see it with fresh eyes. If you're itching to write before then and have time to do so, write something else. The time away from your novel will give you distance.

Some writers give their first draft to a writers' group or to alpha readers—meaning readers who see your draft in all its messiness. I don't use alpha readers because that keeps me from writing quickly and moving forward in the first draft. If I know someone—anyone—is going to read it, I feel compelled to at least change major issues like point of view or missing scenes. So my first draft is for my eyes only.

Whether you seek comments from others or rely solely on yourself, I highly recommend reading the first draft on paper. It looks different than it does on screen, and reading on paper engages a different part of your brain. Both those factors help you see your work more objectively.

As you read, write notes to yourself either in the margins or in a separate document about major changes you need. By major, I mean changes to the actions or motivations of your main characters, point-of-view changes, and/or reorganization of scenes to make your plot points occur at the right stage, to change the plot points, or to significantly alter the story in some other way.

Once you've made those changes, go back on screen and look at the actual writing. Now is the time to focus on each scene. Ask yourself again if the POV is the best one, whether your description of the physical location and characters brings your reader into the scene, whether you can use more of the senses (it's easy to rely too much on sight and hearing and neglect smell, touch, and taste), and whether the characters' emotions are coming through.

After you've rewritten to address those points, send your draft to beta readers. These are readers who look at the manuscript when it's near-finished and comment on it as a whole. You can use friends, but beware, they may not feel free enough to give you objective advice. You can also find beta readers in writers' forums.

If you have the funds to pay a developmental editor, that person will look at your manuscript, or an outline, or both for the overall story arc and give you advice. (If you plan to do this, you should shop for an editor ahead of time and find out at what stage that person is most effective. She or he might recommend that you send an earlier draft.) While my beta readers are reading my manuscript, I forbid myself from looking at it. That way when I review their comments and look again at the manuscript, it's easier to see the flaws.

Once you make any changes based on the comments and your next review, you'll need to have your manuscript copyedited and proofread so there won't be errors when you publish it or submit it to agents or publishers. If you don't have the funds, you may be able to work out a barter system with other writers. Just be sure whoever proofreads and edits has a good track record. (Ask authors whose work you like for recommendations.) I've known writers who paid editors, only to end up with a book full of errors anyway.

You should also do your own proofreading. But

remember, it's very hard to spot errors in your own work, as you've read it too many times. So always have at least one other pair of eyes look it over.

15

WHEN IT'S OVER

Finishing your first novel, and every novel after that, is exciting, and it's a great accomplishment. Which is why you may feel a bit let down afterward. You've devoted so much time and energy to this story and these characters. Unless you're doing a series, they will no longer be part of your everyday life. If you are writing a series, they still won't be part of your life in the same way. It can feel like losing your friends.

So be prepared. Plan what you'll write next, so you have a new project to be excited about. Plan to do things you enjoy that you might have set aside or spent less time on so you could write, whether it's seeing more movies, playing sports, or hanging out more with people you love.

It also can be scary to send your novel into the world. Whether or not your book is autobiographical, you are sharing a lot of yourself in it. Publishing it or seeking a publishing contract or an agent risks rejection, whether from agents, publishing houses, or readers who might post negative reviews.

Also, the reactions of friends, family, and colleagues can be a source of happiness or stress. (From experience, it'll probably be both.) Some people you thought would be thrilled for you will shrug it off as if it's no big deal or, worse, go out of their way to belittle your effort or your finished product. But others whom you never imagined were interested in writing or in you will ask you all kinds of questions, be excited for you, and show tremendous support.

The thing to remember is that you've accomplished something huge, regardless of whether or how you publish your novel. Think of all the people who say, "Oh, I want to write a book someday." Most of them never do. You did. That's awesome!

If you'd like to read more about plot or about character development, check out my books The One-Year Novelist: A Week-By-Week Guide To Writing Your Novel In One Year; **Buffy And The**

Art Of Story Season One: Writing Better Fiction By Watching Buffy; and **Creating Compelling Characters From The Inside Out** or listen to my podcast **Buffy and the Art of Story.**

I also offer individual feedback on your novel's plot and personal story coaching. Or, for those who prefer online self-study courses, I created **How To Plot Your Novel: From Idea To First Draft.** You can find out more at **Help With Your Novel** on the website WritingAsASecondCareer.com.

Whatever stage you're at, planning, finished, or in between, thank you for letting me be part of your journey, and good luck with your next steps.

> Join the Writing As A Second Career email list if you'd like to receive updates on new releases, sales, writing and marketing tips, and your free Super Simple Story Structure worksheets.
>
> **Did you enjoy this book and find it helpful?**
>   Please write a review to help others find out about it. Even a sentence or a few words can make a difference.

ALSO BY L. M. LILLY

The One-Year Novelist: A Week-By-Week Guide To Writing Your Novel In One Year

Creating Compelling Characters From The Inside Out

Write On: How To Overcome Writer's Block So You Can Write Your Novel

Happiness, Anxiety, and Writing: Using Your Creativity To Live A Calmer, Happier Life

Buffy And The Art Of Story Season One: Writing Better Fiction By Watching Buffy

Buffy And The Art Of Story Season Two Part 1

Buffy And The Art Of Story Season Two Part 2

How To Write A Novel, Grades 6-8

As Lisa M. Lilly:

The Awakening (Book 1 in The Awakening Series)

The Unbelievers (Book 2 in The Awakening Series)

The Conflagration (Book 3 in The Awakening Series)

The Illumination (Book 4 in The Awakening Series)

The Complete Awakening Supernatural Thriller Series Box Set

When Darkness Falls (a standalone supernatural suspense novel)

The Tower Formerly Known As Sears And Two Other Tales Of Urban Horror

The Worried Man (Q.C. Davis Mystery 1)

The Charming Man (Q.C. Davis Mystery 2)

The Fractured Man (Q.C. Davis Mystery 3)

The Troubled Man (Q.C. Davis Mystery 4)

The Hidden Man (Q.C. Davis Mystery 5)

Q.C. Davis Mysteries 1-3 (The Worried Man, The Charming Man, and The Fractured Man) Box Set

ABOUT THE AUTHOR

An author, lawyer, and adjunct professor of law, L. M. Lilly's non-fiction includes The One-Year Novelist: A Week-By-Week Guide To Writing Your Novel In One Year; *Happiness, Anxiety, and Writing: Using Your Creativity To Live A Calmer, Happier Life; Buffy And The Art Of Story Season One: Writing Better Fiction By Watching Buffy*; and *Creating Compelling Characters From The Inside Out.*

Writing as Lisa M. Lilly, she is the author of the bestselling Awakening supernatural thriller series about Tara Spencer, a young woman who becomes the focus of a powerful religious cult when she mysteriously finds herself pregnant, and of the Q.C. Davis mystery series, a traditional detective series set in Lilly's hometown of Chicago. She is currently working on the latest book in that series.

Lilly also is the author of **When Darkness Falls**, a gothic horror novel set in Chicago's South Loop, and the short-story collection **The Tower**

Formerly Known as Sears and Two Other Tales of Urban Horror, the title story of which was made into the short film Willis Tower.

She is the host of the podcast **Buffy and the Art of Story.** Find the podcast and her fiction at LisaLilly.com.

www.WritingAsASecondCareer.com
lisa@lisalilly.com